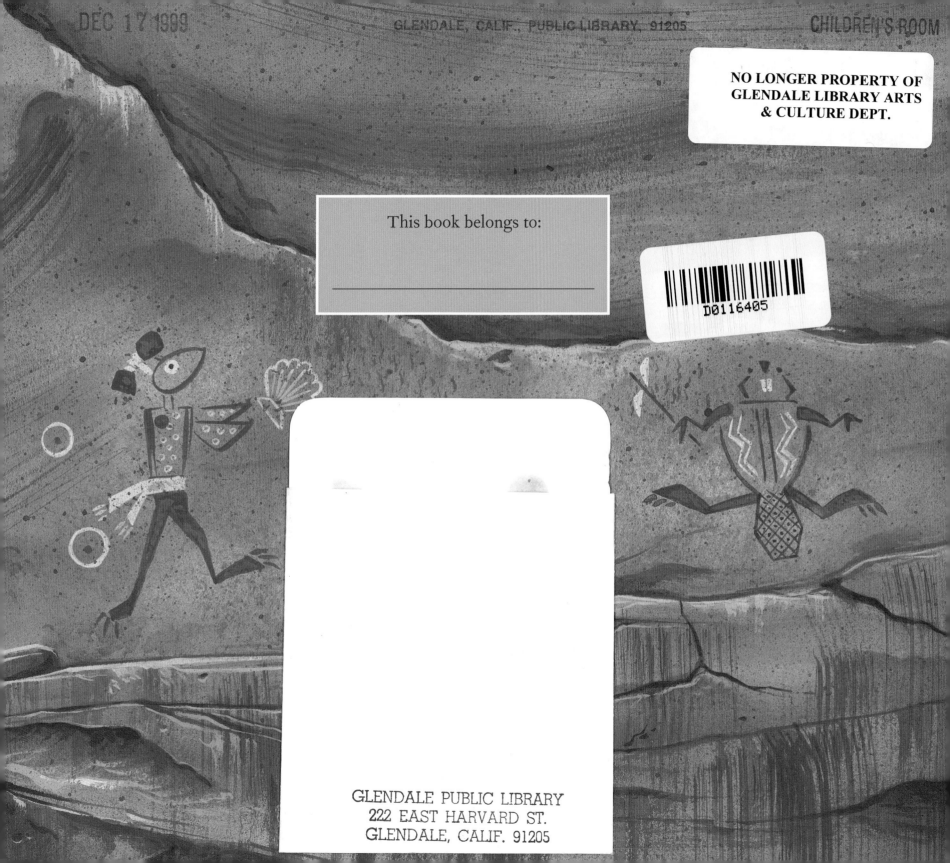

Snail Girl Brings Water

A Navajo Story

RETOLD BY *Geri Keams*

ILLUSTRATED BY *Richard Ziehler-Martin*

rising moon

Books for Young Readers from Northland Publishing

To Don for being a loving companion on the warriors' journey.—G.K.

To my wife, Paige, for her patience, and to Kayleigh and Rory for their inspiration.—R.Z.

The illustrations were done in acrylic on illustration board
The text type was set in Fournier
The display type was set in Truesdell
Composed in the United States of America
Designed by Trina Stahl
Cover designed by Billie Jo Bishop
Art Directed by Jennifer Schaber
Edited by Erin Murphy and Aimee Jackson
Production Supervised by Lisa Brownfield

Manufactured in China by Palace Press International

FIRST IMPRESSION
ISBN 0-87358-622-X

Library of Congress Catalog Card Number 98-18609
Keams, Geri.
Snail girl brings water : a Navajo story / by Geri Keams ;
illustrated by Richard Ziehler-Martin.
p.   cm.
Summary: A retelling of a traditional Navajo creation myth which explains how water came to earth.
ISBN 0-87358-662-X
1. Navajo mythology. 2. Water—Southwest, New—Folklore. 3. Creation—Mythology—Southwest, New.
[1. Navajo Indians—Folklore. 2. Indians of North America—Southwest, New-Folklore. 3. Water—Folklore.
4. Creation—Folklore. 5. Folklore—Southwest, New.] I. Ziehler-Martin, Richard, ill. II. Title.
E99.N3K3245 1998
398.2'089'972-dc21   98-18609

0607/7.5M/9-98

A Note from the Author

AS A CHILD growing up in the Painted Desert of Arizona, I was taught the importance of water-catching tales, stories about how water came to our world. From listening to these stories, I learned that water is precious and that we all have to take care of it. In my homeland, where there is very little rainfall, we live by the messages in these stories. I hope you learn from the message of *Snail Girl Brings Water*. You will most likely never see Snail in the same way. Enjoy.

*L*ONG AGO, it is said, there was a mighty flood, and the People left their world, the Fourth World, the Underworld, and came up into the Fifth World, the world we live in today. They found themselves on the shore of a great ocean.

The People broke into groups by clan and went out to find new homes. But at the end of four days, they came back to the place by the ocean.

"There's no fresh water to drink in this world," they said. They stood by the biggest body of water they had ever seen, but it was salty and they couldn't drink it without getting sick. "What are we going to do?" they asked.

First Woman stood in front of the People and spoke. "Someone will have to go back down to the old world below, back through the hole from which we emerged, to find some fresh water. If I could have just a little water, I could sing my water song and make many streams and rivers grow."

First Woman was the first human being ever made. She was tall with strong arms and hands and a gentle, kind face. Her eyes shone with wisdom and strength. She looked at the People, and her eyes fell on the group that was the Water Clan.

"One of you should go," she said. "You should have brought the water with you when we left the old world."

Then First Woman made a beautiful water bottle out of sea shells. She put a stopper made of red coral in the opening and she wove some rainbow into a loop to carry it. When she finished, she held it up in front of her and faced the Water Clan.

"So, who will go?" she asked.

Out of the group came two Animal People, Otter and Beaver. Long, long ago, before the world was finished, they say there were Animal People. Otter and Beaver walked upright on two legs, but they had wide tails like paddles, just like the tails they wear today, and they were great warriors.

Otter said, "We're from the Water Clan. We're the best swimmers, and we should be the ones to go."

First Woman smiled at them proudly. She hung the water bottle around Otter's neck. Together, Otter and Beaver jumped into the water. They went down, down, down until they reached the bottom and walked along the ocean floor.

Soon they came to a valley of water lilies. There were lilies of every color. It was so beautiful that Otter and Beaver decided to stop.

Beaver said, "We should take some of these flowers and plant them in our new world!"

"Good idea," Otter agreed.

So Otter put down the bottle, and soon they were both covered from head to toe in water lilies, roots, and vines. When they had gathered all they could, they journeyed back to the world above.

When they came out of the water, the People waiting on the beach were amazed. Otter and Beaver looked like two trees coming out of the ocean.

"It's us!" Otter yelled.

The people cried, "Otter and Beaver have come back!" Everyone was excited.

"Look what we found!" Beaver said. "We're going to plant these here in our new home!"

First woman anxiously waited for the water bottle.

Otter pulled and tugged at the roots and vines. "I've got it," he said. "It's here somewhere." But he looked and looked and couldn't find it.

"You have it, Cousin Beaver," Otter said. Together they pulled and tugged on the vines and flowers, but they didn't find the bottle.

"Oh, no!" Otter cried. "I think we forgot it . . . down there . . . " Otter's voice got smaller as he realized what they had done.

First Woman's eyes narrowed. "This won't do at all. You two go away from here. I don't want to see you for awhile."

So Beaver and Otter waddled away, dragging their tails between their legs, to plant their vines and flowers. Today we know that Otter and Beaver still surround themselves with water lilies and roots and vines.

"We still don't have any fresh water," First Woman said. She looked at the Water Clan and noticed Frog and Turtle standing tall and proud among the others. "You two. You must go into the ocean and find the water bottle. Then you must find the hole leading to the Fourth World and bring back some pure water."

Frog and Turtle were the finest young warriors in the clan. They were also known as the most handsome. All of the women wanted to marry them.

"We'll help our cousins," Turtle said.

"We'll find that water bottle," Frog said.

They jumped into the water and went down, down, down to the land at the bottom. They walked along the sand until they reached the valley of water lilies. Turtle saw a piece of rainbow in the sand. He reached down and pulled out the water bottle and tied it to his back.

Together Frog and Turtle journeyed down into canyons and over mountains until Turtle was so tired that he plopped down.

"I can't walk another step," Turtle groaned. "My back is sore. It feels like the water bottle has worn a hole in my back!"

Frog looked at him and said, "Turtle, there is a hole in your back!"

Turtle moaned, "Frog, you go on without me. I'm going to wait here." And he wouldn't budge.

"All right," Frog said. "You rest." And he tied the water bottle to his back and disappeared over the next hill.

Turtle sat and rested. Then he had an idea. Turtle was an artist, and he liked to make things. He found some seashells and began to put them together like pieces of a puzzle. He used some vines and seaweed to string them together, and he put them on

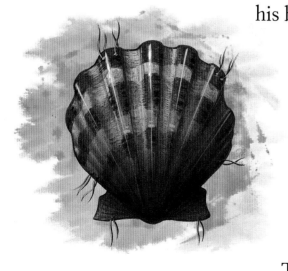

his back in one big piece. He knocked on it, and it was solid as rock. Then he had another idea. He gathered some lighter-colored shells, put them together into another big piece, and hung it on his front. He attached it to the back at the shoulders and the knees.

"Hey!" Turtle said. "Shell armor!" He started to bubble with excitement. His arms and legs went in and out of his shell armor as he danced his first Turtle dance.

In the meantime, Frog was getting tired, too. He found some bluish, greenish water. "This looks clean enough," he said, and he filled up the bottle.

The water bottle was so heavy that by the time Frog returned to Turtle, his knees had risen up to his shoulders and his eyes were bulging out of his head.

"What happened to you?" Turtle asked.

"Get this thing off me! It's so heavy that I can't stand up straight!" yelled Frog.

"I'll carry the bottle," Turtle said. "It can't hurt my back anymore—look, shell armor!"

Turtle tied the bottle around his new shell armor. Together Frog and Turtle went back up through the water to the world above, where the People waited for them.

The people admired Turtle's shell armor and giggled at Frog's bulgy eyes. First Woman opened the water bottle and out came algae, bugs, worms, and seaweed. The water had turned brown.

"Oh, no!" First Woman cried. "This isn't pure spring water. This is ocean water." She touched her finger to the coral stopper and tasted the water. "It's salty! You should have tasted it first!"

"It looked clean to me," Frog shrugged.

"You two go away from here," First Woman said. "I don't want to see you for awhile."

Turtle and Frog sadly walked away. And to this day, Turtle has shell armor and Frog's eyes bulge out of his head.

First Woman was growing weary of the Water Clan's mistakes. She was not used to being this upset. "We still don't have any fresh water," she said.

Someone tugged on her dress. First Woman looked down and saw a thin little girl with long, raven-black hair.

"I am Snail," the child said in a small, squeaky voice. "I'm from the Water Clan, and I'd like to help my people. I want to go get the water."

First Woman looked at the People and the People looked at each other. Everyone knew that Snail was the slowest swimmer of the Water Clan. Nobody thought she would make it, but nobody else wanted to go. First Woman nodded. "You are very brave, Snail," she said. And she tied the bottle to Snail Girl's back. Snail slowly slipped into the great waters. She went down, down, down to the land at the bottom, her long black hair flowing behind her.

Snail Girl went past the valley of water lilies, past the
place where Turtle gathered the shells for his armor,
past the place where Frog had gotten the
seawater. Finally, Snail came to a hole
in the sand with bubbles coming
out of it. She went into the
darkness of this hole,
deeper and deeper, back
to the Fourth World.
There she found some
pure water. She tasted
it, and it was delicious
and fresh. There was
just enough to fill up the
water bottle. She carefully placed
the coral stopper tightly in the bottle.
She went back up through the hole and made
her journey home.

The full moon was shining when Snail Girl came out of the water. She had been gone for such a long time that no one waited for her at the seashore.

Slowly, Snail Girl walked up the hill where she made her home. She was so tired that she didn't feel the rainbow loop coming loose and the water bottle falling off her back. She was so worn out that she didn't hear the bottle dragging in the dirt and rocks. She was so sleepy that she didn't notice the water trickling out.

Snail Girl went to her home and took the bottle off her back. She looked at it and couldn't believe her eyes. There was a hole in the bottom of the bottle.

"Oh no! It's empty!" she cried.

She was so exhausted that she couldn't even cry. She fell to the ground fast asleep.

First Woman woke up from a dream. "I dreamed Snail has returned!" she whispered. First Woman believed in the power of dreams.

She ran down to the ocean's edge. She followed Snail Girl's trail up the hill. Halfway up she saw something shining at her feet in the moonlight. She stopped and reached down to touch it. It was wet. She tasted it. "Fresh water!" she said, and she breathed a sigh of relief. "Snail did it!"

Long ago, they say, everyone had a magic song. First Woman began to sing her magic song, and the small drops of pure water began to grow. They turned into a trickle at first, then a stream, then a river. The river got longer and wider and deeper and faster, and soon the biggest river anybody had ever seen rushed into the ocean.

First Woman looked at the river and smiled, and then she remembered Snail.

First Woman ran to Snail Girl's home and woke her up. Snail opened her weary eyes and saw it was First Woman, and she said, "All the water is gone. Look at the bottle. There's a hole in it." She began to cry.

But First Woman's eyes lit up. "Come with me, Snail," she said, and they went outside. A beautiful river ran down the hill to the ocean.

"You did it, Snail," First Woman said. "You carried the water all the way back from the old world, and even though a hole wore through the bottle as you walked up the hill, I got here in time to take a seed of water and make it grow." Snail smiled.

Snail Girl and First Woman stood together near the top of the hill and watched the sun rise over the river. As the People awoke and came out of their homes, they were amazed at what they saw. They whooped and hollered with joy and happiness.

The people held a giving thanks ceremony. Everyone sat in a circle, and Snail was the Honored One.

First Woman spoke. "Snail, you are very brave, and we thank you. From this day on, you will carry the water bottle on your back as a symbol of your great journey. You will leave a trail of moisture behind you every place you travel. This will be a message to everyone that our pure water is precious and we must take care of it."

And so it was from that day on.

GERI KEAMS was born in the Painted Desert of the Navajo Nation in Arizona, and belongs to the Streak-of-Black-Forest Clan. The eldest of nine brothers and sisters, Geri grew up herding sheep, helping her grandmother weave, and listening to the stories of the elders. She now shares her stories throughout the country in museums, libraries, schools, and colleges and her poetry appears in several anthologies. Geri received a degree in drama education from the University of Arizona and is now an accomplished actress (best know for her role in the classic Western *The Outlaw Josey Wales*, starring Clint Eastwood) who has served as a cultural consultant on several movies and televison programs, including Disney's *Pocahontas* and several episodes of *The X-Files*. Geri tells the stories of Native American people in order to encourage others to explore Native cultures rather than accept stereotypes. Native legends, creation stories, and chants should be kept alive, Geri says, "for all to hear, learn, and to honor the earth, our mother."

RICHARD ZIEHLER-MARTIN lives in Pasadena, California, with his wife and their two children. He has a BFA in Painting from the University of Arizona and a BFA in Illustration from the Art Center College of Design in Pasadena, California. Richard has spent the last eleven years as an artist in the animation industry, including working for Warner Bros./Disney and Universal Cartoon Studios, as well as numerous other studios. In 1994, Richard was nominated for a Daytime Emmy Award for outstanding achievement in animation for *Where on Earth Is Carmen San Diego?* (Fox TV Studios). Richard grew up as a child of Park Service parents, living on the Crow Reservation in Montana at Little Bighorn Battlefield, and in Arizona at Tuzigoot National Monument. Richard's love for Native American art and culture grew out of his early childhood experiences and has been with him ever since. Illustrator and author came together by a happy twist of fate when Richard invited Geri Keams to tell her stories at his daughter's birthday party. When Richard learned that Geri was looking for an illustrator for her book *Snail Girl Brings Water*, he eagerly volunteered.